S0-CRE-389

WAKE UP & PLAY

Illustrated by Russell Spina

Disney PRESS

NEW YORK

KELLY

FIRST EDITION 1 3 5 7 9 10 8 6 4 2

Library of Congress Catalog Card Number: 91-71344

ISBN: 1-56282-055-9

Contents

Good Morning to You

Good morning to you.
Good morning to you.
Good morning, dear baby,
Good morning to you.

This Is the Way

This is the way we brush our hair,
Brush our hair, brush our hair.
This is the way we brush our hair
So early in the morning.

This is the way we wash our face,
Wash our face, wash our face.
This is the way we wash our face
So early in the morning.

This is the way we brush our teeth,
Brush our teeth, brush our teeth.
This is the way we brush our teeth
So early in the morning.

Where Is Thumbkin?

Where is Thumbkin, where is Thumbkin?
Here I am, here I am,
How are you this morning?
Very well, I thank you.
Run a-way, run a-way.

The Eensy Weensy Spider

The eensy weensy spider
Went up the water spout.
Down came the rain
And washed the spider out.
Out came the sun
And dried up all the rain.
And the eensy weensy spider
Went up the spout again.

Old MacDonald

Old MacDonald had a farm, E-I-E-I-O!
And on this farm he had some chicks, E-I-E-I-O!
With a chick-chick here, and a chick-chick there
Here a chick, there a chick, everywhere a chick-chick!
Old MacDonald had a farm, E-I-E-I-O!

Old MacDonald had a farm, E-I-E-I-O!
And on this farm he had a cow, E-I-E-I-O!
With a moo-moo here, and a moo-moo there
Here a moo, there a moo, everywhere a moo-moo!
Chick-chick here, and a chick-chick there
Here a chick, there a chick, everywhere a chick-chick!
Old MacDonald had a farm, E-I-E-I-O!

Old MacDonald had a farm, E-I-E-I-O!
And on this farm he had some ducks, E-I-E-I-O!
With a quack-quack here, and a quack-quack there
Here a quack, there a quack, everywhere a quack-quack!
Moo-moo here, and a moo-moo there
Here a moo, there a moo, everywhere a moo-moo!
Chick-chick here, and a chick-chick there
Here a chick, there a chick, everywhere a chick-chick!
Old MacDonald had a farm, E-I-E-I-O!

Old MacDonald had a farm, E-I-E-I-O!
And on this farm he had some pigs, E-I-E-I-O!
With an oink-oink here, and an oink-oink there
Here an oink, there an oink, everywhere an oink-oink!
Quack-quack here, and a quack-quack there
Here a quack, there a quack, everywhere a quack-quack!
Moo-moo here, and a moo-moo there
Here a moo, there a moo, everywhere a moo-moo!
Chick-chick here, and a chick-chick there
Here a chick, there a chick, everywhere a chick-chick!
Old MacDonald had a farm, E-I-E-I-O!

Yankee Doodle

Yankee Doodle went to town
Upon a little pony.
He stuck a feather in his hat,
And called it Macaroni.

Yankee Doodle, keep it up,
Yankee Doodle dandy.
Mind the music and the step,
and with the girls be handy.

London Bridge

London Bridge is falling down,
Falling down, falling down.
London Bridge is falling down,
My fair lady.

London Bridge is half built up....
London Bridge is all built up....
Take the key and lock her up....

Ring-a-Round-a-Rosy

Ring-a-round-a-rosy,
A pocket full of posies,
Ashes! Ashes!
We all fall down.

Mary Had a Little Lamb

Mary had a little lamb,
Little lamb, little lamb,
Mary had a little lamb,
Its fleece was white as snow.
And everywhere that Mary went,
Mary went, Mary went,
Everywhere that Mary went,
The lamb was sure to go.

Jack and Jill

Jack and Jill went up the hill,
To fetch a pail of water,
Jack fell down and broke his crown,
And Jill came tumbling after.

The Caterpillar

Fuzzy little caterpillar,
Crawling, crawling on the ground.
Fuzzy little caterpillar,
Nowhere, nowhere to be found.
Tho' we've looked and looked and hunted,
Ev'ry where around!

When the little caterpillar
Found his furry coat too tight,
Then a snug cocoon he made him,
Spun of silk so soft and light;
Rolled himself away within it—
Slept there day and night.

See how this cocoon is stirring—
Now a little head we spy.
What is this our caterpillar,
Spreading gorgeous wings to dry?
Soon the free and happy creature
Flutters gaily by.

The Farmer in the Dell

The farmer in the dell,
The farmer in the dell,
Heigh-ho, the derry-o,
The farmer in the dell.

The farmer takes a wife....
The wife takes a child....
The child takes a nurse....
The nurse takes a dog....
The dog takes a cat....
The cat takes a rat....
The rat takes the cheese....
The cheese stands alone....

Three Blind Mice

Three blind mice, three blind mice,
See how they run, see how they run.
They all ran after the farmer's wife,
Who cut off their tails with a carving knife,
Did ever you see such a sight in your life
As three blind mice!

Pat-a-Cake

Pat-a-cake, pat-a-cake, baker's man,
Bake me a cake as fast as you can.
Pat it and prick it and mark it with a B,
And put it in the oven for Baby and me.

I'm a Little Teapot

I'm a little teapot, short and stout,
Here is my handle, here is my spout.

When I get all steamed up, I just shout,
Tip me over and pour me out.

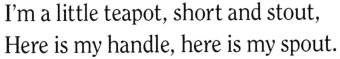

This Old Man

This old man, he played one
He played knick-knack on my thumb

CHORUS
With a knick-knack, patty-whack
Give a dog a bone
This old man came rolling home

This old man, he played two
He played knick-knack on my shoe
CHORUS

This old man, he played three
He played knick-knack on my knee
CHORUS

This old man, he played four
He played knick-knack on my door
CHORUS

This old man, he played five
He played knick-knack on my hive
CHORUS

This old man, he played six
He played knick-knack on my sticks
CHORUS

This old man, he played seven
He played knick-knack up to heaven
CHORUS

This old man, he played eight
He played knick-knack on my gate
CHORUS

This old man, he played nine
He played knick-knack on my line
CHORUS

This old man, he played ten
He played knick-knack over again

With a knick-knack, patty-whack
Give a dog a bone
This old man came rolling home

Do Your Ears Hang Low?

Do your ears hang low,

Do they wobble to and fro?

Can you tie them in a knot,

Can you tie them in a bow?

Can you throw them over your shoulder,
Like a Continental soldier,

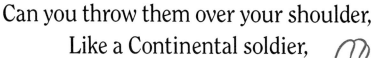

Do your ears hang low?

Head, Shoulders, Knees and Toes

Head, shoulders, knees and toes, knees and toes,

Head, shoulders, knees and toes, knees and toes,

Eyes and ears and mouth and nose,

Head, shoulders, knees and toes, knees and toes.

Round and Round the Garden

Round and round the garden,
Like a teddy bear.
One step,
Two step,
And tickly under there!

See-Saw, Marjorie Daw

See-saw, Marjorie Daw,
Johnny shall have a new master.
He shall have but a penny a day,
Because he can't work any faster.

Row, Row, Row Your Boat

Row, row, row your boat
Gently down the stream,
Merrily, merrily, merrily, merrily,
Life is but a dream.

This Little Piggy

This little piggy went to market,

This little piggy stayed home,

This little piggy had roast beef,

This little piggy had none.

This little piggy cried, "Wee-wee-wee,"
All the way home.

Twinkle, Twinkle, Little Star

Twinkle, twinkle, little star,
How I wonder what you are,
Up above the world so high,
Like a diamond in the sky.
Twinkle, twinkle, little star,
How I wonder what you are.